THE 30-MI\RE

HENRY IV, PART 1

✳

"Nick Newlin's work as a teaching artist for Folger Education during the past thirteen years has provided students, regardless of their experience with Shakespeare or being on stage, a unique opportunity to tread the boards at the Folger Theatre. Working with students to edit Shakespeare's plays for performance at the annual Folger Shakespeare Festivals has enabled students to gain new insights into the Bard's plays, build their skills of comprehension and critical reading, and just plain have fun working collaboratively with their peers.

Folger Education promotes performance-based teaching of Shakespeare's plays, providing students with an interactive approach to Shakespeare's plays in which they participate in a close reading of the text through intellectual, physical, and vocal engagement. Newlin's *The 30-Minute Shakespeare* series is an invaluable resource for teachers of Shakespeare, and for all who are interested in performing the plays."

ROBERT YOUNG, PH.D.
DIRECTOR OF EDUCATION
FOLGER SHAKESPEARE LIBRARY

Henry IV, Part 1: The 30-Minute Shakespeare
ISBN 978-1-935550-11-2
Adaptation, essays, and notes © 2010 by Nick Newlin

Cover design by Sarah Juckniess
Printed in the United States of America

Distributed by Consortium Book Sales & Distribution
www.cbsd.com

NICOLO WHIMSEY PRESS
www.30MinuteShakespeare.com

Art Director: Sarah Juckniess
Managing Editors: Katherine Little, Leah Gordon

THE FIRST PART of

HENRY THE FOURTH

WITH THE LIFE AND DEATH of HENRY

THE 30-MINUTE SHAKESPEARE

Written by WILLIAM SHAKESPEARE

Abridged AND Edited

by NICK NEWLIN

Nicolo Whimsey
Press

Brandywine, MD

To Leo Bowman
A caring and
dedicated teacher

Special thanks to Joanne Flynn, Bill Newlin, Eliza Newlin Carney, William and Louisa Newlin, Michael Tolaydo, Hilary Kacser, Sarah Juckniess, Katherine Little, Eva Zimmerman, Leah Gordon, Julie Schaper and all of Consortium, Leo Bowman and the students, faculty, and staff at Banneker Academic High School, and Robert Young Ph.D., and the Folger Shakespeare Library, especially the wonderful Education Department.

✳ TABLE OF CONTENTS

✳ NO EXPERIENCE NECESSARY

I was not a big "actor type" in high school, so if you weren't either, or if the young people you work with are not, then this book is for you. Whether or not you work with "actor types," you can use this book to stage a lively and captivating thirty-minute version of a Shakespeare play. No experience is necessary.

When I was about eleven years old, my parents took me to see Shakespeare's *Two Gentlemen of Verona*, which was being performed as a Broadway musical. I didn't comprehend every word I heard, but I was enthralled with the language, the characters, and the story, and I understood enough of it to follow along. From then on, I associated Shakespeare with *fun*.

Of course Shakespeare is fun. The Elizabethan audiences knew it, which is one reason he was so popular. It didn't matter that some of the language eluded them. The characters were passionate and vibrant, and their conflicts were compelling. Young people study Shakespeare in high school, but more often than not they read his work like a text book and then get quizzed on academic elements of the play, such as plot, theme, and vocabulary. These are all very interesting, but not nearly as interesting as standing up and performing a scene! It is through performance that the play comes alive and all its "academic" elements are revealed. There is nothing more satisfying to a student or teacher than the feeling of "owning" a Shakespeare play, and that can only come from performing it.

But Shakespeare's plays are often two or more hours long, making the performance of an entire play almost out of the question. One can perform a single scene, which is certainly a good start, but what about the story? What about the changes a character goes through as the play progresses? When school groups perform one scene unedited, or when they lump several plays together, the audience can get lost. This is why I have always preferred to tell the story of the play.

The 30-Minute Shakespeare gives students and teachers a chance to get up on their feet and act out a Shakespeare play in half an hour, using his language. The emphasis is on key scenes, with narrative bridges between scenes to keep the audience caught up on the action. The stage directions are built into this script so that young actors do not have to stand in one place; they can move and tell the story with their actions as well as their words. And it can all be done in a classroom during class time!

That is where this book was born: not in a research library, a graduate school lecture, a professional stage, or even an after-school drama club. All of the play cuttings in *The 30-Minute Shakespeare* were first rehearsed in a D.C. public high school English class, and performed successfully at the Folger Shakespeare Library's annual Secondary School Shakespeare Festival. The players were not necessarily "actor types." For many of them, this was their first performance in a play.

Something almost miraculous happens when students perform Shakespeare. They "get" it. By occupying the characters and speaking the words out loud, students gain a level of understanding and appreciation that is unachievable by simply reading the text. That is the magic of a performance-based method of learning Shakespeare, and this book makes the formerly daunting task of staging a Shakespeare play possible for anybody.

With *The 30-Minute Shakespeare* book series I hope to help teachers and students produce a Shakespeare play in a short amount of time, thus jump-starting the process of discovering the beauty, magic, and fun of the Bard. Plot, theme, and language reveal themselves through the performance of these half-hour play cuttings, and everybody involved receives the priceless gift of "owning" a piece of Shakespeare. The result is an experience that is fun and engaging, and one that we can all carry with us as we play out our own lives on the stages of the world.

NICK NEWLIN
Brandywine, MD
March 2010

CHARACTERS IN THE PLAY

The following is a list of the characters that appear in this cutting of Henry IV, Part 1.

Twenty-five actors performed in the original production. This number can be increased to about thirty or decreased to about twelve by having actors share or double roles.

For the full breakdown of characters, see Sample Program.

FALSTAFF: Sir John Falstaff, a debauched and witty aristocrat

PRINCE HENRY: Also called Harry or Hal; oldest son to King Henry IV

POINS: Companion to Falstaff; gentleman-in-waiting to Prince Henry

GADSHILL: Companion to Falstaff

BARDOLPH: Companion to Falstaff

PETO: Companion to Falstaff

TRAVELER ONE

TRAVELER TWO

HOSTESS: Mistress Quickly, hostess of the Boar's Head Tavern in Eastcheap

MORTIMER: Edmund Mortimer, Earl of March; brother to Lady Percy, husband to Lady Mortimer

GLENDOWER: Owen Glendower, a Welsh rebel; father to Lady Mortimer

HOTSPUR: Henry Percy, nicknamed Hotspur; son to Earl of Northumberland

LADY MORTIMER: Daughter to Glendower, wife to Mortimer

LADY PERCY: Wife to Hotspur, sister to Mortimer

KING HENRY IV: Father to Prince Henry; formerly Henry of Bollingbroke

EARL OF DOUGLAS: Archibald, Earl of Douglas; a Scottish noble

LANCASTER: Prince John of Lancaster, also called the Duke of Lancaster; third son to King Henry IV

From King Henry IV, Part 2 *(final scene in this cutting):*

PISTOL: An irregular humorist; Falstaff's henchman

SHALLOW: Robert Shallow, a country justice of the peace

KING HENRY V: Formerly Prince Henry; newly crowned king

LORD CHIEF-JUSTICE: Attendant to King Henry V; nemesis of Falstaff

ATTENDANT

NARRATOR

✳ **SCENE 1.** (ACT I, SCENE II)

Eastcheap. The Boar's-Head Tavern.

SOUND OPERATOR *plays* Sound Cue #1 ("Merry tavern music").

STAGEHANDS *move bench to center stage, downstage of pillars.*

Enter **NARRATOR** *from stage right, coming downstage center.*

NARRATOR
> Young Prince Henry—called "Harry" or "Hal" by
> his friends—carouses in the tavern in Eastcheap
> with the fat knight Jack Falstaff and other friends,
> including Poins, Hal's gentleman-in-waiting. Hal
> and Poins devise a plan to rob Falstaff and company
> of their stolen money, just for fun and mockery.

Enter **FALSTAFF** *from stage right.*

FALSTAFF *lies down on bench on his back, falls asleep, and
starts snoring loudly.* **PRINCE HENRY** *enters, looks at* **FALSTAFF**
amusedly, and tickles the sleeping man's nose with his hat.
FALSTAFF *sputters and wakes up, a bit disoriented.*

FALSTAFF
> Now, Hal, what time of day is it, lad?

PRINCE HENRY *(slaps* **FALSTAFF** *on the belly with his hat; moves
> behind him)*
> Thou art so fat-witted, with drinking of old sack that
> thou hast forgotten to demand that truly which thou

wouldst truly know. What a devil hast thou to do with the time of the day; unless hours were cups of sack and minutes capons?

FALSTAFF *roll up to a sitting position, stands, and moves a few steps stage left.* PRINCE HENRY *lies down on bench on his side, facing* FALSTAFF.

FALSTAFF
>Marry, then, sweet wag, when thou art king, let not us that are squires of the night's body be called thieves of the day's beauty: let us be Diana's foresters, gentlemen of the shade, minions of the moon.

FALSTAFF *moons* PRINCE HENRY.

PRINCE HENRY *(covers his face in fright)*
>Thou sayest well, and it holds well too; for the fortune of us that are the moon's men doth ebb and flow like the sea, being governed, as the sea is, by the moon.

FALSTAFF *(joins* PRINCE HENRY *on bench; slaps him on the back)*
>Thou hast the most unsavory similes and art indeed the most comparative, rascalliest, sweet young prince, and art indeed able to corrupt a saint. Thou hast done much harm upon me, Hal; God forgive thee for it!

PRINCE HENRY
>Where shall we take a purse tomorrow, Jack?

FALSTAFF
>'Zounds, where thou wilt, lad.

Enter POINS *from stage right.*

>Poins!

PRINCE HENRY

Good morrow, Ned!

POINS

Good morrow, sweet Hal. What says Monsieur Remorse?

POINS squeezes in between **PRINCE HENRY** *and* **FALSTAFF** *on bench.*

What says Sir John Sack and Sugar?

POINS gives **FALSTAFF** *a friendly shove and* **FALSTAFF** *nearly falls over.* **POINS** *then puts his arms around* **PRINCE HENRY** *and* **FALSTAFF** *conspiratorially.*

My lads, my lads, to-morrow morning, by four o'clock, early at Gadshill! There are pilgrims going to Canterbury with rich offerings, and traders riding to London with fat purses: If you will go, I will stuff your purses full of crowns; if you will not, tarry at home and be hanged. *(to* **FALSTAFF***)* Sir John, I prithee, leave the prince and me alone: I will lay him down such reasons for this adventure that he shall go.

FALSTAFF *(stands)*

Farewell; you shall find me in Eastcheap.

PRINCE HENRY

Farewell, thou latter spring! Farewell, All-hallown summer!

Exit **FALSTAFF** *stage right.*

POINS

Now, my good sweet honey lord, ride with us to-morrow: I have a jest to execute that I cannot manage alone. Falstaff, Bardolph, Peto, and Gadshill shall

rob those men that we have already waylaid: yourself
and I will not be there; and when they have the booty,
if you and I do not rob them, cut this head off from
my shoulders. I know them to be as true-bred cowards
as ever turned back; the virtue of this jest will be, the
incomprehensible lies that this same fat rogue will tell
us when we meet at supper: how thirty, at least, he
fought with; and in the reproof of this lies the jest.

PRINCE HENRY
> Well, I'll go with thee.

POINS
> Farewell, my lord.

Exit POINS *stage right.*

PRINCE HENRY
> Herein will I imitate the sun,
> Who doth permit the base contagious clouds
> To smother up his beauty from the world,
> That, when he please again to be himself,
> Being wanted, he may be more wonder'd at,
> So, when this loose behavior I throw off *(stands)*
> And pay the debt I never promised,
> By how much better than my word I am,
> By so much shall I falsify men's hopes;
> And like bright metal on a sullen ground,
> My reformation, glittering o'er my fault,
> Shall show more goodly and attract more eyes
> Than that which hath no foil to set it off.
> I'll so offend, to make offense a skill;
> Redeeming time when men think least I will.

Exit PRINCE HENRY *stage right.*

STAGEHANDS *remove bench.*

✳ **SCENE 2.** (ACT II, SCENE II)

The highway, near Gadshill.

Enter NARRATOR *from stage right, coming downstage center.*

NARRATOR
> Falstaff and his band of rogues rob the travelers, but their plan backfires.

Exit NARRATOR *stage left.*

Enter PRINCE HENRY *and* POINS *from stage right; they stand near stage right pillar.*

POINS
> Come, shelter, shelter: I have removed Falstaff's horse, and he frets like a gummed velvet.

PRINCE HENRY
> Stand close.

Enter FALSTAFF, *looking for Poins, whom he does not see.*

FALSTAFF
> Poins! Poins, and be hanged! Poins!

PRINCE HENRY *(comes up behind* FALSTAFF*)*
> Peace, ye fat-kidneyed rascal! What a brawling dost thou keep!

FALSTAFF *jumps and squeals from fright; he then pretends not to have reacted that way.*

FALSTAFF

Where's Poins, Hal? The rascal hath removed my horse, and tied him I know not where. A plague upon it when thieves cannot be true one to another! *(loudly)* Give me my horse, you rogues.

Enter GADSHILL, PETO, *and* BARDOLPH *from stage right, walking in a line with* GADSHILL *leading. They all bump into each other and slap the person behind them with their hats. Since* BARDOLPH *is last, he can't slap anybody; this frustrates him, so he slaps his bottle instead.*

GADSHILL

Stand.

FALSTAFF

So I do, against my will.

BARDOLPH

There's money of the king's coming down the hill.

PRINCE HENRY

Sirs, you four shall front them in the narrow lane; Ned Poins and I will walk lower: if they 'scape from your encounter, then they light on us.

PETO

How many be there of them?

GADSHILL

Some eight or ten.

FALSTAFF
>'Zounds, will they not rob us?

PRINCE HENRY
>What, a coward, Sir John Paunch?

FALSTAFF
>Indeed, I am not John of Gaunt, your grandfather;
>but yet no coward, Hal.

PRINCE HENRY (*whispering to* POINS)
>Ned, where are our disguises?

POINS
>Here, hard by: stand close.

Exit PRINCE HENRY *and* POINS *stage right.*

FALSTAFF
>Now, every man to his business.

Enter TRAVELERS *from stage left.*

TRAVELER ONE
>Come, neighbor: the boy shall lead our horses down
>the hill; we'll walk afoot awhile, and ease our legs.

FALSTAFF
>Stand!

TRAVELER TWO
>Jesus bless us!

FALSTAFF
>Strike; down with them; bacon-fed knaves!
>Fleece them.

TRAVELER TWO

    O, we are undone, both we and ours for ever!

FALSTAFF

    Ye fat chuffs: on, bacons, on!

FALSTAFF, GADSHILL, *and* **PETO** *rob and bind* **TRAVELERS.**
BARDOLPH *mistakenly is tied up as well and led out with them; he yells muffled protestations through the scarf tied around his mouth. Exit* **ALL** *stage left.*

Re-enter **PRINCE HENRY** *and* **POINS** *from stage right.*

PRINCE HENRY

    The thieves have bound the true men. Now could
    thou and I rob the thieves and go merrily to
    London, it would be argument for a week, laughter
    for a month and a good jest for ever.

POINS

    Stand close; I hear them coming.

PRINCE HENRY *and* **POINS** *hide behind stage left pillar.*

Re-enter **FALSTAFF, GADSHILL, PETO,** *and* **BARDOLPH** *from stage left.*

FALSTAFF

    Come, my masters, let us share.

PRINCE HENRY *and* **POINS** *leap out from behind stage left pillars, brandishing swords.*

PRINCE HENRY

    Your money!

POINS

    Villains!

FALSTAFF, GADSHILL, PETO, *and* BARDOLPH *drop the money and run screaming, with* FALSTAFF *screaming the loudest.* HAL *and* POINS *laugh hysterically, nearly falling down from the effort.*

PRINCE HENRY
> Got with much ease. Now merrily to horse:
> Falstaff lards the lean earth as he walks along:
> Were't not for laughing, I should pity him.

POINS
> How the rogue roar'd!

Exit POINS *and* PRINCE HENRY *stage right.*

✳ SCENE 3. (ACT II, SCENE IV)

Eastcheap. The Boar's-Head Tavern.

STAGEHANDS *move table stage center, placing one stool stage right of table and one stool stage left.*

Enter **NARRATOR** *from stage right, coming downstage center.*

NARRATOR
> Prince Hal teases Falstaff about his cowardice. Falstaff and Hal take turns role-playing the king, with revealing results.

Exit **NARRATOR** *stage left.*

Enter **PRINCE HENRY** *and* **POINS** *from stage right.* **PRINCE HENRY** *sits in stool stage left and* **POINS** *stands behind table.*

PRINCE HENRY
> Falstaff and the rest of the thieves are at the door: shall we be merry?

POINS
> As merry as crickets, my lad.

Enter **FALSTAFF, GADSHILL, PETO,** *and* **BARDOLPH** *from stage right, carrying wine.* **BARDOLPH** *pours a small cup for* **PRINCE HENRY,** *swigs from the bottle, and then pulls a flask out of his pocket and swigs from that. He then pulls a smaller bottle from another pocket, swigs from it, and burps.*

FALSTAFF *sits on a stool and the others stand around table behind him.*

FALSTAFF
> A plague of all cowards! There be four of us here have ta'en a thousand pound this day morning.

PRINCE HENRY
> Where is it, Jack? Where is it? *(pretends to look for the money)*

FALSTAFF
> Where is it! Taken from us it is: a hundred upon poor four of us. I have 'scaped by miracle.

FALSTAFF *stands and mimes getting stabbed eight times in the chest, then four times in the legs.*

> I am eight times thrust through the doublet, four through the hose; my sword hacked like a hand-saw—ecce signum! *(shows his mangled sword)* A plague of all cowards!

FALSTAFF *toasts, drinks, then refills his cup.* BARDOLPH *does so as well, three times in a row, until* PETO *shoots him a look and grabs the bottle from him.*

PRINCE HENRY
> Why, thou clay-brained guts, thou knotty-pated fool. We two saw you four set on four and bound them, and were masters of their wealth. Then did we two set on you four; and, with a word, out-faced you from your prize, and have it; *(holds up bag of money)* and, Falstaff, you carried your guts away with quick dexterity, and roared for mercy. What device canst thou now find out to hide thee from this shame?

POINS

Come, let's hear, Jack; what trick hast thou now?

FALSTAFF *(pauses; thinks)*

Why, hear you, my masters: was it for me to kill the true prince? I am as valiant as Hercules, but beware instinct. I was now a coward on instinct. I am glad you have the money.

PRINCE HENRY *(to* **FALSTAFF***)*

You fought fair; so did you, Peto; so did you, Bardolph:

GADSHILL *feels left out and points to himself.*

You are lions too, you ran away upon instinct, you will not touch the true prince.

BARDOLPH

'Faith, I ran when I saw others run. *(burps)*

FALSTAFF

Tell me, Hal, art thou not horribly afraid?

PRINCE HENRY

Not a whit, i' faith; I lack some of thy *(pauses)* instinct.

FALSTAFF

Well, thou wert be horribly chid tomorrow when thou comest to thy father: if thou love me, practice an answer.

PRINCE HENRY *(playfully)* Do thou stand for my father, and examine me upon the particulars of my life.

FALSTAFF

> Shall I? Content: this chair shall be my state, this
> dagger my scepter, and this cushion my crown.
> *(puts cushion on head)* Here is my speech. Stand
> aside, nobility.

HOSTESS

> O Jesu, this is excellent sport, i' faith! O, the father,
> how he holds his countenance! He doth it as like one
> of these harlotry players as ever I see!

HOSTESS *laughs until people look at her in irritation; she stops.*

FALSTAFF *(addresses* PETO, *then* BARDOLPH*)*
> Peace, good pint-pot; peace, good tickle-brain.

FALSTAFF *composes himself, breathes deeply, and gets into character.*

FALSTAFF

> Harry, I do not only marvel where thou spendest thy
> time, but also the company thou keepest:

FALSTAFF *looks at the group before him, who protest vocally.*

> and yet there is a virtuous man whom I have often
> noted in thy company, but I know not his name.

PRINCE HENRY
> What manner of man, your majesty?

FALSTAFF *(looks at his belly)*
> A goodly portly man, i' faith, and of a cheerful look,
> and, as I think, his age some fifty,

HOSTESS *and others interrupt by yelling, "Sixty!"*

or, by'r lady, inclining to three score; His name is
Falstaff: Harry, I see virtue in his looks. Falstaff: him
keep with, the rest banish.

PRINCE HENRY
Do thou stand for me, and I'll play my father.

FALSTAFF
Depose me?

FALSTAFF *and* PRINCE HENRY *switch places.* PRINCE HENRY *sits in
the stool and takes the dagger and cushion from* FALSTAFF *while*
FALSTAFF *stands.*

PRINCE HENRY
Well, here I am set.

FALSTAFF
And here I stand: judge, my masters.

PRINCE HENRY
Now, Harry, whence come you?

FALSTAFF *(kneels)*
My noble lord, from Eastcheap.

PRINCE HENRY
The complaints I hear of thee are grievous.

FALSTAFF
'Sblood, my lord, they are false.

PRINCE HENRY
Swearest thou, ungracious boy? Thou art violently
carried away from grace: there is a devil haunts thee
in the likeness of an old *(pauses)* fat *(pauses)* man.

(*stares at* FALSTAFF) Why dost thou converse with that trunk of humors,

With each insult, the crowd at the tavern responds verbally.

that bolting-hutch of beastliness, that stuffed cloak-bag of guts, with the pudding in his belly. Wherein is he good, but to taste sack and drink it? Wherein villanous, but in all things?

The cheering dies down, as it seems PRINCE HENRY *is being unnecessarily mean.*

Wherein worthy, but in nothing?

The cheering fades away completely. The crowd is a little uncomfortable.

FALSTAFF
Whom means your grace?

PRINCE HENRY
That villanous abominable misleader of youth, Falstaff, that old white-bearded Satan.

FALSTAFF (*less jolly, more timid*)
My lord, the man I know.

PRINCE HENRY
I know thou dost.

FALSTAFF
If to be old and merry be a sin, then many an old host that I know is damned: No, my good lord; banish Peto, banish Bardolph, banish Poins: but for sweet Jack Falstaff, kind Jack Falstaff, true Jack Falstaff, being, as he is, old Jack Falstaff, banish not

him thy Harry's company, banish plump Jack, and
banish all the world.

PRINCE HENRY
I do, I will.

PRINCE HENRY *stands and begins to leave, looking and acting
more like a king than when he came in. Exit* PRINCE HENRY *stage
rear as all look on.*

Exit POINS, GADSHILL, *and* PETO *stage right.* HOSTESS *wakes*
BARDOLPH, *who has fallen asleep, and leads him off stage right.*

FALSTAFF *looks out over the audience, sighs, and lumbers off
stage right.*

STAGEHANDS *remove table.*

✳ SCENE 4. (ACT III, SCENE I)

The Archdeacon's house.

Enter NARRATOR *from stage right, coming downstage center.*

NARRATOR
> Hot-headed Harry Percy—known as Hotspur—
> tangles with the Welsh Lord Glendower as they plan
> to divide up the kingdom they intend to conquer.

Exit NARRATOR *stage right.*

Enter HOTSPUR, MORTIMER, *and* GLENDOWER *from stage left.*

MORTIMER
> These promises are fair, the parties sure,
> And our induction full of prosperous hope.

HOTSPUR
> Lord Mortimer, and cousin Glendower,
> Will you sit down?

GLENDOWER *sits on stage right stool and* MORTIMER *sits in stool stage left.* HOTSPUR *remains standing.*

> A plague upon it! I have forgot the map.

GLENDOWER
> No, here it is. *(pulls out map)*
> Sit, cousin Percy; sit, good cousin Hotspur,
> At my birth the frame and huge foundation of the earth
> Shaked like a coward.

HOTSPUR
O, then the earth shook to see the heavens on fire,
And not in fear of your nativity.

MORTIMER *stands between* PERCY *and* GLENDOWER *and separates them with his hands.*

MORTIMER
Peace, cousin Percy; you will make him mad.

GLENDOWER
Three times hath Henry Bolingbroke made head
Against my power; thrice have I sent him
Bootless home and weather-beaten back.

HOTSPUR
Home without boots, and in foul weather too!

GLENDOWER
Come, here's the map: shall we divide our right
According to our threefold order ta'en?

GLENDOWER *sets the map on the ground.* ALL *examine it.*

MORTIMER
The archdeacon hath divided it
Into three limits very equally:

HOTSPUR (*points at map with a stick*)
Methinks my moiety, north from Burton here,
In quantity equals not one of yours:
See how this river cuts me from the best of all
    my land.
It shall not wind with such a deep indent,
To rob me of so rich a bottom here.

GLENDOWER
> Not wind? It shall, it must; you see it doth.

HOTSPUR (*stands*)
> Who shall say me nay?

GLENDOWER
> Why, that will I.

GLENDOWER *and* HOTSPUR *take a step closer to each other and stare at each other for a moment.* GLENDOWER *looks away first.*

> Come, you shall have Trent turn'd.

HOTSPUR.
> Are the indentures drawn? Shall we be gone?

GLENDOWER
> The moon shines fair; you may away by night.

Exit GLENDOWER *stage right.*

MORTIMER
> Fie, cousin Percy! How you cross my father!

HOTSPUR
> I cannot choose: sometime he angers me.
> O, he is as tedious as a railing wife.

MORTIMER *sits* HOTSPUR *in the stool to calm him down.*

MORTIMER
> In faith, my lord, you are too wilful-blame.

HOTSPUR
> Well, I am school'd: Here come our wives, and let us
> take our leave.

Re-enter GLENDOWER *with* LADY MORTIMER *and* LADY PERCY *from stage right.*

MORTIMER *and* PERCY *gaze lovingly at their respective wives as they enter.*

HOTSPUR
> Come, Kate, thou art perfect in lying down:
> come, quick, quick, that I may lay my head in thy lap.

LADY PERCY
> Go, ye giddy goose.

LADY PERCY *sits and* HOTSPUR *lays his head in her lap.*

SOUND OPERATOR *plays* Sound Cue #2 ("Welsh music").

GLENDOWER *conducts the music, as if summoning it from thin air;* ALL *listen, enraptured.*

HOTSPUR
> Now I perceive the devil is a good musician.

LADY PERCY
> Then should you be nothing but musical
> for you are altogether governed by humors.
> Lie still, ye thief,
> Now God help thee!

HOTSPUR
> To the Welsh lady's bed.

LADY PERCY
> What's that?

HOTSPUR

Peace. Come, Kate, I'll have your song too.

LADY PERCY

Not mine, in good sooth.

Exit HOTSPUR *and* LADY PERCY *stage left, giggling.*

GLENDOWER

Come, come, Lord Mortimer; you are as slow
As hot Lord Percy is on fire to go.

MORTIMER *stands and helps* LADY MORTIMER *to her feet.*

Exit MORTIMER *and* LADY MORTIMER *stage right, arm in arm.*
GLENDOWER *watches them leave for a few moments, then exits
stage right.*

STAGEHANDS *remove stools, then place throne center.*

✳ **SCENE 5** (ACT III, SCENE II)

London. The palace.

Enter NARRATOR *from stage right, coming downstage center.*

NARRATOR
>Prince Hal reconciles with his father, King Henry IV,
>by swearing to fight the rebels and to defeat Hotspur.

Exit NARRATOR *stage right.*

Enter KING HENRY IV *and* PRINCE HENRY *from stage left.*
KING HENRY IV *sits on the throne.*

KING HENRY IV
>I know not whether God will have it so,
>For some displeasing service I have done,
>But thou dost in thy passages of life
>Make me believe that thou art only mark'd
>For the hot vengeance and the rod of heaven
>To punish my mistreadings. Tell me else,
>Could such inordinate and low desires,
>Such barren pleasures, rude society,
>As thou art match'd withal and grafted to,
>Accompany the greatness of thy blood
>And hold their level with thy princely heart?

PRINCE HENRY
>So please your majesty
>Find pardon on my true submission. *(kneels)*

KING HENRY IV

    God pardon thee! Yet let me wonder, Harry,
    At thy affections, which do hold a wing
    Quite from the flight of all thy ancestors.
    The hope and expectation of thy time
    Is ruin'd. Harry, thou has lost thy princely privilege
    With vile participation: not an eye
    But is a-weary of thy common sight,
    Save mine, which hath desired to see thee more.

PRINCE HENRY *(touched and surprised)*

    I shall hereafter be more myself.

KING HENRY IV

    For all the world
    Percy now leads ancient lords and reverend bishops on
    To bloody battles and to bruising arms.
    Thrice hath this Hotspur, Mars in swathling clothes,
    Discomfited great Douglas, ta'en him once,
    And what say you to this? Percy, Northumberland,
    The Archbishop's grace of York, Douglas, Mortimer,
    Capitulate against us and are up.

PRINCE HENRY *(stands; walks slowly downstage center)*

    I will redeem all this on Percy's head
    And in the closing of some glorious day
    Be bold to tell you that *(turns to* KING HENRY IV*)*
        I am your son;
    For the time will come,
    That I shall make this northern youth exchange
    His glorious deeds for my indignities. *(kneels again)*
    This, in the name of God, I promise here:
    And I will die a hundred thousand deaths
    Ere break the smallest parcel of this vow.

KING HENRY IV *stands and helps* PRINCE HENRY *to his feet. They hold a long handshake and eye contact.*

KING HENRY IV
A hundred thousand rebels die in this:
Thou shalt have charge and sovereign trust herein.

Exit KING HENRY IV *stage right.* PRINCE HENRY *follows.*

STAGEHANDS *remove throne.*

✳ SCENE 6. (ACT V, SCENE IV)

A field between the camps.

Enter NARRATOR *from stage right, coming downstage center.*

NARRATOR
> We are on the battlefield. True colors are revealed,
> with Hal showing bravery and loyalty, and Falstaff
> showing that he is, well, still a coward and a liar.
> (But, somehow, a loveable one!)

Exit NARRATOR *stage left.*

Enter KING HENRY IV *and* EARL OF DOUGLAS *from stage right, bearing swords.*

EARL OF DOUGLAS
> Another king! They grow like Hydra's heads:
> I am the Douglas, fatal to all those
> That wear those colors on them: what art thou,
> That counterfeit'st the person of a king?

KING HENRY IV
> The king himself; I will assay thee: so, defend thyself.

EARL OF DOUGLAS *(examines* KING HENRY IV*)*
> I fear thou art another counterfeit;
> And yet, in faith, thou bear'st thee like a king:
> But mine I am sure thou art, whoe'er thou be,
> And thus I win thee.

KING HENRY IV *and* EARL OF DOUGLAS *fight. With* KING HENRY IV *in danger,* PRINCE HENRY *enters from stage left.*

PRINCE HENRY
> Hold up thy head, vile Scot, it is the Prince of Wales
> that threatens thee.

PRINCE HENRY *joins the fight.* KING HENRY IV *is fatigued, but fights* EARL OF DOUGLAS *valiantly.* EARL OF DOUGLAS *escapes offstage right.* PRINCE HENRY *runs to check on his father.*

PRINCE HENRY
> Cheerly, my lord how fares your grace?

KING HENRY IV
> Stay, and breathe awhile:
> Thou hast redeem'd thy lost opinion,
> And show'd thou makest some tender of my life,
> In this fair rescue thou hast brought to me.

PRINCE HENRY
> O God! They did me too much injury
> That ever said I hearken'd for your death.

KING HENRY IV *and* PRINCE HENRY *meet each other's gaze for a brief emotional moment.*

Exit KING HENRY IV *stage left.*

Enter HOTSPUR *from stage right.*

HOTSPUR
> If I mistake not, thou art Harry Monmouth.
> My name is Harry Percy.

PRINCE HENRY
> I am the Prince of Wales.

HOTSPUR
> The hour is come
> To end the one of us;
> I can no longer brook thy vanities.

PRINCE HENRY IV and HOTSPUR fight.

Enter FALSTAFF from stage left.

FALSTAFF
> Well said, Hal! To it Hal! Nay, you shall find no boy's
> play here, I can tell you.

*Re-enter EARL OF DOUGLAS; he fights with FALSTAFF, who falls
down as if he were dead.*

Exit EARL OF DOUGLAS stage right.

HOTSPUR is wounded; he falls.

HOTSPUR
> O, Harry, thou hast robb'd me of my youth!
> Percy, thou art dust
> And food for—

HOTSPUR dies.

PRINCE HENRY
> For worms, brave Percy: fare thee well, great heart!

PRINCE HENRY sees FALSTAFF on the ground.

> What, old acquaintance! Could not all this flesh
> Keep in a little life? Poor Jack, farewell!

Exit PRINCE HENRY *stage right.*

FALSTAFF *continues to appear dead; after a few moments, he rises up suddenly.*

FALSTAFF

> The better part of valor is discretion; in the which
> better part I have saved my life. 'Zounds, I am afraid
> of this gunpowder Percy, though he be dead: how, if
> he should counterfeit too and rise? Therefore, sirrah,

FALSTAFF *stabs* HOTSPUR *in the thigh.*

> with a new wound in your thigh, come you along
> with me.

FALSTAFF *begins to drag* HOTSPUR *offstage.*

Enter PRINCE HENRY *and* LANCASTER *from stage right.* FALSTAFF *stops.*

LANCASTER

> But, soft! Whom have we here?
> Did you not tell me this fat man was dead?

PRINCE HENRY

> I did; I saw him dead. Art thou alive?
> Or is it fantasy that plays upon our eyesight?

FALSTAFF

> No, that's certain; I am not a double man: *(glances
> at his belly)* but if I be not Jack Falstaff, then am I a
> Jack. There is Percy:

FALSTAFF *gestures to* HOTSPUR'S *body.*

if your father will do me any honor, so; if not, let
him kill the next Percy himself. I look to be either
earl or duke, I can assure you.

PRINCE HENRY
Why, Percy I killed myself and saw thee dead.

FALSTAFF
Didst thou? Lord, Lord, how this world is given
to lying! I grant you I was down and out of breath;
and so was he: but we rose both at an instant and
fought a long hour by Shrewsbury clock. I gave him
this wound in the thigh: if the man were alive and
would deny it, 'zounds, I would make him eat a
piece of my sword.

LANCASTER
This is the strangest tale that ever I heard.

PRINCE HENRY
This is the strangest fellow, brother John.

SOUND OPERATOR *plays* Sound Cue #3 ("Trumpet retreat").

The trumpet sounds retreat; the day is ours.

Exit **PRINCE HENRY** *and* **LANCASTER** *stage right.*

FALSTAFF
If I do grow great, I'll grow less; for I'll purge, and
leave sack, and live cleanly as a nobleman should do.

Exit **FALSTAFF** *stage right, dragging* **HOTSPUR'S** *body by the legs.*

✳ SCENE 7. (FALSTAFF'S SPEECH: ACT V, SCENE I. ADDITIONAL MATERIAL FROM *HENRY IV, PART 2:* ACT V, SCENE V)

Enter NARRATOR *from stage right, coming downstage center.*

NARRATOR
> Time has passed, and Hal is now King Henry V.
> He rejects Falstaff as part of the former life that he
> now renounces.

Exit NARRATOR *stage left.*

Enter FALSTAFF, SHALLOW, PISTOL, *and* BARDOLPH *from stage right. As usual,* BARDOLPH *bumps into the man in front of him.* ALL *stand in a line, side by side, watching for the royal parade.*

FALSTAFF
> Stand here by me, Master Robert Shallow; I will
> make the king do you grace: I will leer upon him as
> a' comes by; and do but mark the countenance that
> he will give me.

PISTOL
> God bless thy lungs, good knight.

FALSTAFF
> Come here, Pistol; stand behind me. This doth show
> my earnestness of affection.

FALSTAFF *puts his arm around* PISTOL'S *shoulders.* PISTOL *in turn puts his arm around* BARDOLPH. BARDOLPH *goes to puts his arm around someone's shoulders, but there is nobody there, so he puts his arm around a wine bottle instead.*

SHALLOW

It doth so.

FALSTAFF

My devotion,—

SHALLOW

It doth, it doth, it doth.

FALSTAFF

As it were, to ride day and night; and not to deliberate, but to stand stained with travel, and sweating with desire to see him; as if there were nothing else to be done but to see him.

Shouts come from within.

SOUND OPERATOR *plays* Sound Cue #4 ("Royal fanfare").

PISTOL

There roar'd the sea, and trumpet-clangor sounds.

Enter KING HENRY V *from stage left accompanied by the* LORD CHIEF-JUSTICE *and* ATTENDANT *holding* KING HENRY V'S *robe.*

FALSTAFF

God save thy grace, King Hal! My royal Hal!

PISTOL

The heavens thee guard and keep, most royal imp of fame!

FALSTAFF

God save thee, my sweet boy!

KING HENRY V

My lord chief-justice, speak to that vain man.

The CHIEF-JUSTICE *tries to think of something to say but can't think of anything; he fumbles over his words, starting and stopping.*

Lord Chief-Justice have you your wits? Know you what 'tis to speak?

FALSTAFF

My king! My Jove! I speak to thee, my heart!

KING HENRY V

I know thee not, old man: fall to thy prayers.

FALSTAFF *is visibly shaken and upset; he kneels, as do* PISTOL *and* BARDOLPH. BARDOLPH *offers a swig from the bottle to* KING HENRY V, *who ignores him.* SHALLOW *gives a small bow.*

How ill white hairs become a fool and jester!
I have long dream'd of such a kind of man,
So surfeit-swell'd, so old and so profane;
But, being awaked, I do despise my dream.
Reply not to me with a fool-born jest:
Presume not that I am the thing I was;
For God doth know, so shall the world perceive,
That I have turn'd away my former self;
So will I those that kept me company.
When thou dost hear I am as I have been,
Approach me, and thou shalt be as thou wast,
The tutor and the feeder of my riots:
Till then, I banish thee, on pain of death,

> Not to come near our person by ten mile.
> Set on.

Exit KING HENRY V *and* ATTENDANT.

FALSTAFF *(to* SHALLOW*)*
> Master Shallow, do not you grieve at this; I shall
> be sent for in private to him: look you, he must
> seem thus to the world: this that you heard was but
> a color.

SHALLOW
> A color that I fear you will die in, Sir John.

FALSTAFF
> Fear no colors: go with me to dinner: come,
> Lieutenant Pistol; come, Bardolph: I shall be sent for
> soon at night.

Exit SHALLOW *and* BARDOLPH *stage right.*

FALSTAFF
> I would 'twere bed-time, Hal, and all well.

PRINCE HENRY'S *voice rings out from offstage, an echo from*
> *the past.*
> Why, thou owest God a death.

ALL *begin to enter and surround* FALSTAFF *as he speaks.*

FALSTAFF
> 'Tis not due yet; I would be loath to pay him before
> his day. What need I be so forward with him that
> calls not on me? Well, 'tis no matter; honor pricks
> me on. Yea, but how if honor prick me off when I
> come on? How then? Can honor set to a leg?

ALL

>No.

FALSTAFF

>Or an arm?

ALL

>No.

FALSTAFF

>Or take away the grief of a wound?

ALL

>No.

FALSTAFF

>What is honor? A word. What is in that word
>honor?

ALL

>Air.

FALSTAFF

>Who hath it? He that died o' Wednesday. Doth he
>feel it?

ALL

>No.

FALSTAFF

>'Tis insensible, then. Yea, to the dead. But will it not
>live with the living?

ALL

>No.

FALSTAFF

Why? Detraction will not suffer it. Therefore I'll none of it.

ALL

Honor is a mere scutcheon.

FALSTAFF

And so ends my catechism.

ALL *hold hands and bow. Exeunt.*

* PERFORMING SHAKESPEARE

BACKGROUND:
HOW *THE 30-MINUTE SHAKESPEARE* WAS BORN

In 1981 I performed a "Shakespeare Juggling" piece called "To Juggle or Not To Juggle" at the first Folger Library Secondary School Shakespeare Festival. The audience consisted of about 200 Washington, D.C. area high school students who had just performed thirty-minute versions of Shakespeare plays for each other and were jubilant over the experience. I was dressed in a jester's outfit, and my job was to entertain them. I juggled and jested and played with Shakespeare's words, notably Hamlet's "To be or not to be" soliloquy, to very enthusiastic response. I was struck by how much my "Shakespeare Juggling" resonated with a group who had just performed Shakespeare themselves. "Getting" Shakespeare is a heady feeling, especially for adolescents, and I am continually delighted at how much joy and satisfaction young people derive from performing Shakespeare. Simply reading and studying this great playwright does not even come close to inspiring the kind of enthusiasm that comes from performance.

Surprisingly, many of these students were not "actor types." A good percentage of the students performing Shakespeare that day were part of an English class which had rehearsed the plays during class time. Fifteen years later, when I first started directing plays in D.C. public schools as a Teaching Artist with the Folger Shakespeare Library, I entered a ninth grade English class as a guest and spent two or three days a week for two or three months preparing students for the Folger's annual Secondary School Shakespeare Festival. I have conducted this annual residency with the Folger ever since.

Every year for seven action-packed days, eight groups of students between grades seven and twelve tread the boards onstage at the Folger's Elizabethan Theatre, a grand recreation of a sixteenth-century venue with a three-tiered gallery, carved oak columns, and a sky-painted canopy.

As noted on the Folger website (www.folger.edu), "The festival is a celebration of the Bard, not a competition. Festival commentators—drawn from the professional theater and Shakespeare education communities—recognize exceptional performances, student directors, and good spirit amongst the students with selected awards at the end of each day. They are also available to share feedback with the students."

My annual Folger Teaching Artist engagement, directing a Shakespeare play in a public high school English class, is the most challenging and the most rewarding thing I do all year. I hope this book can bring you the same rewards.

GETTING STARTED: GAMES

How can you get an English class (or any other group of young people, or even adults) to start the seemingly daunting task of performing a Shakespeare play? You have already successfully completed the critical first step, which is buying this book. You hold in your hand a performance-ready, thirty-minute cutting of a Shakespeare play, with stage directions to get the actors moving about the stage purposefully. But it's a good idea to warm the group up with some theater games.

One good initial exercise is called "Positive/Negative Salutations." Students stand in two lines facing each other (four or five students in each line) and, reading from index cards, greet each other, first with a "Positive" salutation in Shakespeare's language (using actual phrases from the plays), followed by a "negative" greeting.

Additionally, short vocal exercises are an essential part of the preparation process. The following is a very simple and effective vocal warm-up: Beginning with the number two, have the whole group count to twenty using increments of two (i.e., "Two, four, six . . ."). Increase the volume slightly with each number, reaching top volume with "twenty," and then decrease the volume while counting back down, so that the students are practically whispering when they arrive again at "two." This exercise teaches dynamics and allows them to get loud as a group without any individual pressure. Frequently during a rehearsal period, if a student is mumbling inaudibly, I will refer back to this exercise as a reminder that we can and often do belt it out!

"Stomping Words" is a game that is very helpful at getting a handle on Shakespeare's rhythm. Choose a passage in iambic pentameter and have the group members walk around the room in a circle, stomping their feet on the second beat of each line:

Two **house**-holds, **both** a-**like** in **dig**-nity
In **fair** Ve-**ro**na **Where** we **lay** our **scene**

Do the same thing with a prose passage, and have the students discuss their experience with it, including points at which there is an extra beat, etc., and what, if anything, it might signify.

I end every vocal warm-up with a group reading of one of the speeches from the play, emphasizing diction and projection, bouncing off consonants, and encouraging the group members to listen to each other so that they can speak the lines together in unison. For variety I will throw in some classic "tongue twisters" too, such as, "The sixth sheik's sixth sheep is sick."

The Folger Shakespeare Library's website (http://www.folger.edu) and their book series *Shakespeare Set Free,* edited by Peggy O'Brien, are two great resources for getting started with a performance-based teaching of Shakespeare in the classroom. The Folger website has numerous helpful resources and activities, many submitted by teachers, for helping a class actively participate in the process of getting to know a Shakespeare play. For more simple theater games, Viola Spolin's *Theatre Games for the Classroom* is very helpful, as is one I use frequently, *Theatre Games for Young Performers*.

HATS AND PROPS

Introducing a few hats and props early in the process is a good way to get the action going. Hats, in particular, provide a nice avenue for giving young actors a non-verbal way of getting into character. In the opening weeks, when students are still holding onto their scripts, a hat can give an actor a way to "feel" like a character. Young actors are natural masters at injecting their own personality into what they wear, and even small choices made with how a hat is worn (jauntily, shadily, cockily, mysteriously) provide a starting point for discussion of specific characters, their traits, and their relationships with other characters. All such discussions always lead back to one thing: the text. "Mining the text" is consistently the best strategy for uncovering the mystery of Shakespeare's language. That is where all the answers lie: in the words themselves.

WHAT DO THE WORDS MEAN?

It is essential that young actors know what they are saying when they recite Shakespeare. If not, they might as well be scat singing, riffing on sounds and rhythm but not conveying a specific meaning. The real question is: What do the words mean? The answer is multifaceted, and can be found in more than one place. The New Folger Library paperback editions of the plays themselves (edited by Barbara Mowat and Paul Werstine, Washington Square Press) are a great resource for understanding Shakespeare's words and passages and "translating" them into modern English. These editions also contain chapters on Shakespeare's language, his life, his theater, a "Modern Perspective," and further reading. There is a wealth of scholarship embedded in these wonderful books, and I make it a point to read them cover to cover before embarking on a play-directing project. At the very least, it is a good idea for any adult who intends to direct a Shakespeare play with a group of students to go through the explanatory notes that appear on the pages facing the text. These explanatory notes are an indispensable "translation tool."

The best way to get students to understand what Shakespeare's words mean is to ask them what they think they mean. Students have their own associations with the words and with how they sound and feel. The best ideas on how to perform Shakespeare often come directly from the students, not from anybody else's notion. If a student has an idea or feeling about a word or passage, and it resonates with her emotionally, physically, or spiritually, then Shakespeare's words can be a vehicle for her feelings. That can result in some powerful performances!

I make it my job as director to read the explanatory notes in the Folger text, but I make it clear to the students that almost "anything goes" when trying to understand Shakespeare. There are no wrong interpretations. Students have their own experiences, with some shared and some uniquely their own. If someone has an association with the phrase "canker-blossom," or if the words make that student or his character feel or act a certain way, then that is the "right" way to decipher it.

I encourage the students to refer to the Folger text's explanatory notes and to keep a pocket dictionary handy. Young actors must attach some meaning to every word or line they recite. If I feel an actor is glossing over a word, I will stop him and ask him what he is saying. If he doesn't know, we will figure it out together as a group.

PROCESS VS. PRODUCT

The process of learning Shakespeare by performing one of his plays is more important than whether everybody remembers his lines or whether somebody misses a cue or an entrance. But my Teaching Artist residencies have always had the end goal of a public performance for about 200 other students, so naturally the performance starts to take precedence over the process somewhere around Dress Rehearsal in the students' minds. It is my job to make sure the actors are prepared—otherwise they will remember the embarrassing moment of a public mistake and not the glorious triumph of owning a Shakespeare play.

In one of my earlier years of play directing, I was sitting in the audience as one of my narrators stood frozen on stage for at least a minute, trying to remember her opening line. I started scrambling in my backpack below my seat for a script, at last prompting her from the audience. Despite her fine performance, that embarrassing moment is all she remembered from the whole experience. Since then I have made sure to assign at least one person to prompt from backstage if necessary. Additionally, I inform the entire cast that if somebody is dying alone out there, it is okay to rescue him or her with an offstage prompt.

There is always a certain amount of stage fright that will accompany a performance, especially a public one for an unfamiliar audience. As a director, I live with stage fright as well, even though I am not appearing on stage. The only antidote to this is work and preparation. If a young actor is struggling with her lines, I make sure to arrange for a session where we run lines over the telephone. I try to set up a buddy system so that students can run lines with their peers, and this often works well. But if somebody does not have a "buddy," I will personally make the time to help out myself. As I assure my students from the outset, I am not going to let them fail or embarrass themselves. They need an experienced leader. And if the leader has experience in teaching but not in directing Shakespeare, then he needs this book!

It is a good idea to culminate in a public performance, as opposed to an in-class project, even if it is only for another classroom. Student actors want to show their newfound Shakespearian thespian skills to an outside group, and this goal motivates them to do a good job. In that respect, "product" is important. Another wonderful bonus to performing a play is that it is a unifying group effort. Students learn teamwork. They learn to give focus to another actor when he is speaking, and to play off of other characters. I like to end each performance with the entire cast reciting a passage in unison. This is a powerful ending, one that reaffirms the unity of the group.

SEEING SHAKESPEARE PERFORMED

It is very helpful for young actors to see Shakespeare performed by a group of professionals, whether they are appearing live on stage (preferable but not always possible) or on film. Because an entire play can take up two or more full class periods, time may be an issue. I am fortunate because thanks to a local foundation that underwrites theater education in the schools, I have been able to take my school groups to a Folger Theatre matinee of the play that they are performing. I always pick a play that is being performed locally that season. But not all group leaders are that lucky. Fortunately, there is the Internet, specifically YouTube. A quick YouTube search for "Shakespeare" can unearth thousands of results, many appropriate for the classroom.

The first "Hamlet" result showed an 18-year-old African-American actor on the streets of Camden, New Jersey, delivering a riveting performance of Hamlet's "The play's the thing." The second clip was from *Cat Head Theatre,* an animation of cats performing Hamlet. Of course, YouTube boasts not just alley cats and feline thespians, but also clips by true legends of the stage, such as John Gielgud and Richard Burton. These clips can be saved and shown in classrooms, providing useful inspiration.

One advantage of the amazing variety of clips available on YouTube is that students can witness the wide range of interpretations for any given scene, speech, or character in Shakespeare, thus freeing them from any preconceived notion that there is a "right" way to do it.

Furthermore, modern interpretations of the Bard may appeal to those who are put off by the "thees and thous" of Elizabethan speech.

By seeing Shakespeare performed either live or on film, students are able to hear the cadence, rhythm, vocal dynamics, and pronunciation of the language, and they can appreciate the life that other actors breathe into the characters. They get to see the story told dramatically, which inspires them to tell their own version.

PUTTING IT ALL TOGETHER: THE STEPS

After a few sessions of theater games to warm up the group, it's time to begin the process of casting the play. Each play cutting in *The 30-Minute Shakespeare* series includes a cast list and a sample program, demonstrating which parts have been divided. Cast size is generally between twenty and thirty students, with major roles frequently assigned to more than one performer. In other words, one student may play Juliet in the first scene, another in the second scene, and yet another in the third. This will distribute the parts evenly so that there is no "star of the show." Furthermore, this prevents actors from being burdened with too many lines. If I have an actor who is particularly talented or enthusiastic, I will give her a bigger role. It is important to go with the grain—one cast member's enthusiasm can be contagious.

I provide the performer of each shared role with a similar head-piece and/or cape, so that the audience can keep track of the characters. When there are sets of twins, I try to use blue shirts and red shirts, so that the audience has at least a fighting chance of figuring it out! Other than these costume consistencies, I rely on the text and the audience's observance to sort out the doubling of characters. Generally, the audience can follow because we are telling the story.

Some participants are shy and do not wish to speak at all on stage. To these students I assign non-speaking parts and technical roles such as sound operator and stage manager. However, I always get everybody on stage at some point, even if it is just for the final group speech, because I want every group member to experience what it is like to be on a stage as part of an ensemble.

CASTING THE PLAY

Young people can be self-conscious and nervous with "formal" auditions, especially if they have little or no acting experience.

I conduct what I call an "informal" audition process. I hand out a questionnaire asking students if there is any particular role that they desire, whether they play a musical instrument. To get a feel for them as people, I also ask them to list one or two hobbies or interests. Occasionally this will inform my casting decisions. If someone can juggle, and the play has the part of a Fool, that skill may come in handy. Dancing or martial arts abilities can also be applied to roles.

For the auditions, I do not use the cut script. I have students stand and read from the Folger edition of the complete text in order to hear how they fare with the longer passages. I encourage them to breathe and carry their vocal energy all the way to the end of a long line of text. I also urge them to play with diction, projection, modulation, and dynamics, elements of speech that we have worked on in our vocal warm-ups and theater games.

I base my casting choices largely on reading ability, vocal strength, and enthusiasm for the project. If someone has requested a particular role, I try to honor that request. I explain that even with a small part, an actor can create a vivid character that adds a lot to the play. Wide variations in personality types can be utilized: if there are two students cast as Romeo, one brooding and one effusive, I try to put the more brooding Romeo in an early lovelorn scene, and place the effusive Romeo in the balcony scene. Occasionally one gets lucky, and the doubling of characters provides a way to match personality types with different aspects of a character's personality. But also be aware of the potential serendipity of non-traditional casting. For example,

I have had one of the smallest students in the class play a powerful Othello. True power comes from within!

Generally, I have more females than males in a class, so women are more likely (and more willing) to play male characters than vice versa. Rare is the high school boy who is brave enough to play a female character, which is unfortunate because it can reap hilarious results.

GET OUTSIDE HELP

Every time there is a fight scene in one of the plays I am directing, I call on my friend Michael Tolaydo, a professional actor and theater professor at St. Mary's College, who is an expert in all aspects of theater, including fight choreography. Not only does Michael stage the fight, but he does so in a way that furthers the action of the play, highlighting character's traits and bringing out the best in the student actors. Fight choreography must be done by an expert or somebody could get hurt. In the absence of such help, super slow-motion fights are always a safe bet and can be quite effective, especially when accompanied by a soundtrack on the boom box.

During dress rehearsals I invite my friend Hilary Kacser. a Washington-area actor and dialect coach for two decades. Because I bring her in late in the rehearsal process, I have her direct her comments to me, which I then filter and relay to the cast. This avoids confusing the cast with a second set of directions. This caveat only applies to general directorial comments from outside visitors. Comments on specific artistic disciplines such as dance, music, and stage combat can come from the outside experts themselves.

If you work in a school, you might have helpful resources within your own building, such as a music or dance teacher who could contribute their expertise to a scene. If nobody is available in your school, try seeking out a member of the local professional theater. Many local performing artists will be glad to help, and the students are usually thrilled to have a visit from a professional performer.

LET STUDENTS BRING THEMSELVES INTO THE PLAY

The best ideas often come from the students themselves. If a young actor has a notion of how to play a scene, I will always give that idea a try. In a rehearsal of *Henry IV, Part 1*, one traveler jumped into the other's arms when they were robbed. It got a huge laugh. This was something that they did on instinct. We kept that bit for the performance, and it worked wonderfully.

As a director, you have to foster an environment in which that kind of spontaneity can occur. The students have to feel safe to experiment. In the same production of *Henry IV*, Falstaff and Hal invented a little fist bump "secret handshake" to use in the battle scene. The students were having fun and bringing parts of themselves into the play. Shakespeare himself would have approved. When possible I try to err on the side of fun because if the young actors are having fun, then they will commit themselves to the project. The beauty of the language, the story, the characters, and the pathos will follow.

There is a balance to be achieved here, however. In that same production of *Henry IV, Part 1*, the student who played Bardolph was having a great time with her character. She carried a leather wineskin around and offered it up to the other characters in the tavern. It was a prop with which she developed a comic relationship. At the end of our thirty-minute *Henry IV, Part 1*, I added a scene from *Henry IV, Part 2* as a coda: The new King Henry V (formerly Falstaff's drinking and carousing buddy Hal) rejects Falstaff, banishing him from within ten miles of the King. It is a sad and sobering moment, one of the most powerful in the play.

But at the performance, in the middle of the King's rejection speech (played by a female student, and her only speech), Bardolph offered her flask to King Henry and got a big laugh, thus not only upstaging the King but also undermining the seriousness and poignancy of the whole scene. She did not know any better; she was bringing herself to the character as I had been encouraging her to do. But it was inappropriate, and in subsequent seasons, if I foresaw something like that happening as an individual joyfully occupied a character, I attempted to prevent it. Some things we cannot predict. Now I make sure to issue a statement warning against changing any of the blocking on show day, and to watch out for upstaging one's peers.

FOUR FORMS OF ENGAGEMENT:
VOCAL, EMOTIONAL, PHYSICAL, AND INTELLECTUAL

When directing a Shakespeare play with a group of students, I always start with the words themselves because the words have the power to engage the emotions, mind, and body. Also, I start with the words in action, as in the previously mentioned exercise, "Positive and Negative Salutations." Students become physically engaged; their bodies react to the images the words evoke. The words have the power to trigger a switch in both the teller and the listener, eliciting both an emotional and physical reaction. I have never heard a student utter the line "Fie! Fie! You counterfeit, you puppet you!" without seeing him change before my eyes. His spine stiffens, his eyes widen, and his fingers point menacingly.

Having used Shakespeare's words to engage the students emotionally and physically, one can then return to the text for a more reflective discussion of what the words mean to us personally. I always make sure to leave at least a few class periods open for discussion of the text, line by line, to ensure that students understand intellectually what they feel viscerally. The advantage to a performance-based teaching of Shakespeare is that by engaging students vocally, emotionally, and physically, it is then much easier to engage them intellectually because they are invested in the words, the characters, and the story. We always start on our feet, and later we sit and talk.

SIX ELEMENTS OF DRAMA: PLOT, CHARACTER, THEME, DICTION, MUSIC, AND SPECTACLE

Over two thousand years ago, Aristotle's *Poetics* outlined six elements of drama, in order of importance: Plot, Character, Theme, Diction, Music, and Spectacle. Because Shakespeare was foremost a playwright, it is helpful to take a brief look at these six elements as they relate to directing a Shakespeare play in the classroom.

PLOT (ACTION)

To Aristotle, plot was the most important element. One of the purposes of *The 30-Minute Shakespeare* is to provide a script that tells Shakespeare's stories, as opposed to concentrating on one scene. In a thirty-minute edit of a Shakespeare play, some plot elements are necessarily omitted. For the sake of a full understanding of the characters' relationships and motivations, it is helpful to make short plot summaries of each scene so that students are aware of their characters' arcs throughout the play. The scene descriptions in the Folger editions are sufficient to fill in the plot holes. Students can read the descriptions aloud during class time to ensure that the story is clear and that no plot elements are neglected. Additionally, there are one-page charts in the Folger editions of *Shakespeare Set Free,* indicating characters' relations graphically, with lines connecting families and factions to give students a visual representation of what can often be complex interrelationships, particularly in Shakespeare's history plays.

Young actors love action. That is why *The 30-Minute Shakespeare* includes dynamic blocking (stage direction) that allows students to tell the story in a physically dramatic fashion. Characters' movements on the stage are always motivated by the text itself.

CHARACTER

I consider myself a facilitator and a director more than an acting teacher. I want the students' understanding of their characters to spring from the text and the story. From there, I encourage them to consider how their character might talk, walk, stand, sit, eat, and drink. I also urge students to consider characters' motivations, objectives, and relationships, and I will ask pointed questions to that end during the rehearsal process. I try not to show the students how I would perform a scene, but if no ideas are forthcoming from anybody in the class, I will suggest a minimum of two possibilities for how the character might respond.

At times students may want more guidance and examples. Over thirteen years of directing plays in the classroom, I have wavered between wanting all the ideas to come from the students, and deciding that I need to be more of a "director," telling them what I would like to see them doing. It is a fine line, but in recent years I have decided that if I don't see enough dynamic action or characterization, I will step in and "direct" more. But I always make sure to leave room for students to bring themselves into the characters because their own ideas are invariably the best.

THEME (THOUGHTS, IDEAS)

In a typical English classroom, theme will be a big topic for discussion of a Shakespeare play. Using a performance-based method of teaching Shakespeare, an understanding of the play's themes develops from "mining the text" and exploring Shakespeare's words and his story. If the students understand what they are saying and how that relates to their characters and the overall story, the plays' themes will emerge clearly. We always return to the text itself. There are a number of elegant computer programs, such as www.wordle.net, that will count the number of recurring words in a passage and illustrate them graphically. For example, if the word "jealousy" comes up more than any other word in *Othello,* it will appear in a larger font. Seeing the words displayed by size in this way can offer up illuminating insights into the interaction between words in the text and the play's themes. Your computer-minded students might enjoy searching for such tidbits. There are more internet tools and websites in the Additional Resources section at the back of this book.

I cannot overstress the importance of acting out the play in understanding its themes. By embodying the roles of Othello and Iago and reciting their words, students do not simply comprehend the themes intellectually, but understand them kinesthetically, physically, and emotionally. They are essentially **living** the characters' jealousy, pride, and feelings about race. The themes of appearance vs. reality, good vs. evil, honesty, misrepresentation, and self-knowledge (or lack thereof) become physically felt as well as intellectually understood. Performing Shakespeare delivers a richer understanding than that which comes from just reading the play. Students can now relate the characters' conflicts to their own struggles.

DICTION (LANGUAGE)

If I had to cite one thing I would like my actors to take from their experience of performing a play by William Shakespeare, it is an appreciation and understanding of the beauty of Shakespeare's language. The language is where it all begins and ends. Shakespeare's stories are dramatic, his characters are rich and complex, and his settings are exotic and fascinating, but it is through his language that these all achieve their richness. This leads me to spend more time on language than on any other element of the performance.

Starting with daily vocal warm-ups, many of them using parts of the script or other Shakespearean passages, I consistently emphasize the importance of the words. Young actors often lack experience in speaking clearly and projecting their voices outward, so in addition to comprehension, I emphasize projection, diction, breathing, pacing, dynamics, coloring of words, and vocal energy. *Theatre Games for Young Performers* contains many effective vocal exercises, as does the Folger's *Shakespeare Set Free* series. Consistent emphasis on all aspects of Shakespeare's language, especially on how to speak it effectively, is the most important element to any Shakespeare performance with a young cast.

MUSIC

A little music can go a long way in setting a mood for a thirty-minute Shakespeare play. I usually open the show with a short passage of music to set the tone. Thirty seconds of music played on a boom box operated by a student can provide a nice introduction to the play, create an atmosphere for the audience, and give the actors a sense of place and feeling.

iTunes is a good starting point for choosing your music. Typing in "Shakespeare" or "Hamlet" or "jealousy" (if you are going for a theme) will result in an excellent selection of aural performance enhancers at the very reasonable price of ninety-nine cents each (or free of charge, see Additional Resources section.) Likewise, fight sounds, foreboding sounds, weather sounds (rain, thunder), trumpet sounds, etc. are all readily available online at affordable cost. I typically include three sound cues in a play, just enough to enhance but not overpower a production. The boom box operator sits on the far right or left of the stage, not backstage, so he can see the action. This also has the added benefit of having somebody out there with a script, capable of prompting in a pinch.

SPECTACLE

Aristotle considered spectacle the least important aspect of drama. Students tend to be surprised at this since we are used to being bombarded with production values on TV and video, often at the expense of substance. In my early days of putting on student productions, I would find myself hamstrung by my own ambitions in the realm of scenic design.

A simple bench or two chairs set on the stage are sufficient. The sense of "place" can be achieved through language and acting. Simple set dressing, a few key props, and some tasteful, emblematic costume pieces will go a long way toward providing all the "spectacle" you need.

In the stage directions to the plays in *The 30-Minute Shakespeare* series, I make frequent use of two large pillars stage left and right at the Folger Shakespeare Library's Elizabethan Theatre. I also have characters frequently entering and exiting from "stage rear." Your stage will have a different layout. Take a good look at the performing space you will be using and see if there are any elements that can be incorporated into your own stage directions. Is there a balcony? Can characters enter from the audience? (Make sure that they can get there from backstage, unless you want them waiting in the lobby until their entrance, which may be impractical.) If possible, make sure to rehearse in that space a few times to fix any technical issues and perhaps discover a few fun staging variations that will add pizzazz and dynamics to your own show.

The real spectacle is in the telling of the tale. Wooden swords are handy for characters that need them. Students should be warned at the outset that playing with swords outside of the scene is verboten. Letters, moneybags, and handkerchiefs should all have plentiful duplicates kept in a small prop box, as well as with a stage manager, because they tend to disappear in the hands of adolescents. After every rehearsal and performance, I recommend you personally sweep the rehearsal or performance area immediately for stray props. It is amazing what gets left behind.

Ultimately, the performances are about language and human drama, not set pieces, props, and special effects. Fake blood, glitter, glass, and liquids have no place on the stage; they are a recipe for disaster, or, at the very least, a big mess. On the other hand, the props that are employed can often be used effectively to convey character, as in Bardolph's aforementioned relationship with his wineskin.

PITFALLS AND SOLUTIONS

Putting on a play in a high school classroom is not easy. There are problems with enthusiasm, attitude, attention, and line memorization, to name a few. As anybody who has directed a play will tell you, it is always darkest before the dawn. My experience is that after one or two days of utter despair just before the play goes up, show day breaks and the play miraculously shines. To quote a recurring gag in one of my favorite movies, *Shakespeare in Love:* "It's a mystery."

ENTHUSIASM, FRUSTRATION, AND DISCIPLINE

Bring the enthusiasm yourself. Feed on the energy of the eager students, and others will pick up on that. Keep focused on the task at hand. Arrive prepared. Enthusiasm comes as you make headway. Ultimately, it helps to remind the students that a "play" is fun. I try to focus on the positive attributes of the students, rather than the ones that drive me crazy. This is easier said than done, but it is important. One season, I yelled at the group two days in a row. On day two of yelling, they tuned me out, and it took me a while to win them back. I learned my lesson; since then I've tried not to raise my voice out of anger or frustration. As I grow older and more mature, it is important for me to lead by example. It has been years since I yelled at a student group. If I am disappointed in their work or their behavior, I will express my disenchantment in words, speaking from the heart as somebody who cares about them and cares about our performance and our experience together. I find that fundamentally, young people want to please, to do well, and to be liked. If there is a serious discipline problem, I will hand it over to the regular classroom teacher, the administrator, or the parent.

LINE MEMORIZATION

Students may have a hard time memorizing lines. In these cases, see if you can pair them up with a "buddy" and existing friend who will run lines with them in person or over the phone after school. If students do not have such a "buddy," I volunteer to run lines with them myself. If serious line memorization problems arise that cannot be solved through work, then two students can switch parts if it is early enough in the rehearsal process. For doubled roles, the scene with fewer lines can go to the actor who is having memorization problems. Additionally, a few passages or lines can be cut. Again, it is important to address these issues early. Later cuts become more problematic as other actors have already memorized their cues. I have had to do late cuts about twice in thirteen years. While they have gotten us out of jams, it is best to assess early whether a student will have line memorization problems, and deal with the problem sooner rather than later.

In production, always keep several copies of the script backstage, as well as cheat sheets indicating cues, entrances, and scene changes. Make a prop list, indicating props for each scene, as well as props that are the responsibility of individual actors. Direct the Stage Manager and an Assistant Stage Manager to keep track of these items, and on show days, personally double-check if you can.

In thirteen years of preparing an inner-city public high school English class for a public performance on a field trip to the Folger Secondary School Shakespeare Festival, my groups and I have been beset by illness, emotional turmoil, discipline problems, stage fright, adolescent angst, midlife crises (not theirs), and all manner of other emergencies, including acts of God and nature. Despite the difficulties and challenges inherent in putting on a Shakespeare play with a group of young people, one amazing fact stands out in my experience. Here is how many times a student has been absent for show day: Zero. Somehow, everybody has always made it to the show, and the show has gone on. How can this be? It's a mystery.

✳ PERFORMANCE NOTES: *HENRY IV, PART 1*

I directed this performance of *Henry IV, Part 1* in 2008 with a group of high school seniors. These notes are the result of my own review of the performance video. They are not intended to be the "definitive" performance notes for all productions of *Henry IV, Part 1*. Your production will be unique to you and your cast. That is the magic of live theater. What is interesting about these notes is that many of the performance details I mention were not part of the original stage directions. They either emerged spontaneously on performance day or were developed by students in rehearsal after the stage directions had been written into the script. Some of these pieces of stage business work like a charm. Others fall flat. My favorites are the ones that arise directly from the students themselves and demonstrate a union between actor and character, as if that individual has become a vehicle for the character he is playing. To witness an eighteen-year-old young woman "become" Falstaff as Shakespeare's words leave her mouth is a memorable moment indeed.

SCENE 1 (ACT I, SCENE II)

As the opening music plays, Falstaff takes the stage to sleep on a bench while the narrator delivers her speech downstage. Simple choices such as the narrator smiling make a big difference. Actors, even those in small roles, have to be aware of the importance of their facial expressions. We are setting a mood. A year after this production, I had a Hamlet who kept smiling during the speech about "how weary, flat, stale, and unprofitable" were all the uses of this life. It undercut the gloom of the words. Likewise, when a narrator describes a merry character or introduces a comic scene, her smiling telegraphs to the audience that fun is happening!

Prince Henry, or Hal, tiptoes on stage to tickle Falstaff with his hat. If he had merely walked on, he would have set a less merry tone. Strong entrances and exits are crucial: how we walk says much about who we are. Upon first being tickled with the feather from Hal's hat, Falstaff is immobile, still sleeping. On the second tickle he wakes up flailing, which gets a good laugh. It would have likely gotten a better laugh on tickle number three. When possible, employ the rule of three in comedy.

On the line, "minions of the moon," Falstaff turns around and "moons" Hal (i.e., sticks his butt out toward him). Hal shields his eyes and gives a little squeal, which adds to the comedy. Every sound that emits from an actor can enhance the comedy. In theatre, our five senses take in the spectacle. Let's give the audience a feast for the senses!

The actress playing Falstaff in this scene was ebullient. Her enthusiasm radiated out through her face and her limbs, and as Falstaff her gestures were generous and grandiose. She would spread her arms out wide and gesticulate with her dagger, jabbing at the air and reveling in the glory of her character's self-importance. And when Falstaff had moments of contrition, she would bury her head in her hands and slump over dejectedly. There were no half-measures for this actress, just as there are none for Falstaff. She grasped his essence and communicated it to the audience with bravura.

Another physically expressive actress played Poins. She skipped onstage, plunked herself down on the bench between Hal and Falstaff, and draped her legs over each of her friends. This corporeal comfort-ableness helped paint a first scene of merriment among fun-loving friends and set the tone for the rest of the play.

Hal adds a serious note to the end of the first scene by directly informing the audience of his intention to "falsify men's hopes" with his loose behavior. Thus we set a tone for the play in this initial scene, but we also introduce the darker, more serious side to Hal's character.

SCENE 2 (ACT II, SCENE II)

Falstaff re-enters, shouting "Poins" at top volume, and when Poins jumps out from behind the pillar, Falstaff is startled and jumps up with a high little squeak, to the delight of the audience. This aspect of Falstaff's personality—outward bravery coupled with inward cowardice—is on full display later in the scene when the "robbers" accost him. Falstaff's initial show of alarm during Poins's entrance foreshadows the full-blown panic he displays when robbed. Thus Falstaff's jumpiness is a motif that recurs in the symphony of the play.

The entrance of Gadshill, Bardolph, and Peto confirms that we are dealing with a bunch of bumblers; when Gadshill stops, Bardolph and Peto bump into each other—and into Falstaff. Having three comic characters enter in a row provides opportunities for physical comedy that can be repeated to greater effect once we establish that we are dealing with fools. When Gadshill tells Falstaff there are eight men heading their way, Falstaff again emits his trademark mousy squeal. Through repetition of mannerisms, we create a crisp, comic character.

When the two travelers enter and are surprised by Falstaff and his men, one of the eighteen-year-old male actors jumps into the arms of the other, and they are tied up and whisked off the stage while the audience howls with delight. Traveler Two (in the arms of Traveler One) looks straight out to the audience, bug-eyed, and declares, "Jesus bless us," with such commitment that the laughs continue until the group has left the stage. The two actors playing the Travelers devised this piece of business on their own and were well rewarded with audience applause. There are no small roles.

SCENE 3 (ACT II, SCENE IV)

The actress playing Bardolph also serves as a stagehand. Most young actors choose to bring set pieces onto the stage in a fairly neutral fashion, but Bardolph brings her chair into the tavern in character, walking slightly stooped and weaving just a bit, as if slightly inebriated. When she exits the stage following her stagehand duties, she looks at the seated Hal and gives a little finger point upward as she scurries off the stage. This gesture did not necessarily signify anything, but it gets a laugh because it was a "character moment." When she returns later in the play to narrate again, she retains her stooped, scurrying gait, thus reinforcing her quirky and endearing character traits. Audiences appreciate well-drawn personae and consistent characters with personality and quirks. I remind young actors that their efforts toward creating a comic or dramatic role will pay off in audience appreciation.

These merry tavern rascals enjoy their lives, especially Falstaff, who uses his dagger and his cup as extensions of his irrepressible self, mock-stabbing himself multiple times with his own knife as he describes his assault, and continually turning to Bardolph to refill his mug, which he slams down on the table after drinking. The supporting characters in this scene are crucial to the painting of an atmosphere of tavern revelry. They must give focus to Falstaff, responding to his tale-telling, both physically and verbally, laughing with Falstaff when he imitates the King, and correcting him loudly when he claims he is only fifty years old.

Then, when Hal, imitating the King, heaps insults onto Falstaff, the group can respond with increasingly loud "ooh"s as Hal mocks Falstaff's eating and drinking habits. However, when Hal arrives at the line, "Wherein worthy, but in nothing?" the revelers realize that there is some meanness and seriousness to his words and become silent. This silence is more pronounced if the responses have been loud and hearty until this point. By the time Falstaff exclaims, "Banish plump Jack, and banish all the world," and Hal replies, "I do, I will," the mood has changed to quiet and grave. This somber moment (foreshadowing the later rejection of Falstaff, in a scene taken from *Henry*

IV, Part 2) needs the raucous merriment that precedes it in order to succeed. It is the dying out of the crowd sounds that makes Hal's final pronouncement so weighty. Nobody laughs.

As it turned out in performance, the progression from boisterous tavern laughter to uncomfortable silence was not a straight line. As Falstaff lists the fellows he wishes to banish in his stead, Poins, upon hearing his name, let out a loud protest of "Hey!" which got the biggest laugh of all. The group mood had already become subdued at this point, so Poins's protest broke the silence and provided comic relief at a serious moment. This is often the case. Laughter is loudest when the circumstances behind it are serious.

SCENE 4 (ACT III, SCENE I)

Young actors love *Henry IV, Part 1* for its generational conflicts. The clash between the older and younger characters is particularly attractive to adolescents and young adults. In this scene, the power struggle between young Hotspur and the older Glendower is especially vivid and rich. Hotspur speaks loudly, spitting his words out in staccato, while the older Glendower's cadence is more measured. By coloring his words, the actor playing Glendower can paint the simmering annoyance beneath his speech as Hotspur challenges him. The conflict reaches its peak with this interchange, as Glendower responds to Hotspur's demand that the river not wind, because it robs him of land:

> **GLENDOWER**
> Not wind? It shall, it must; you see it doth.

> **HOTSPUR** *(standing)*
> Who shall say me nay?

> **GLENDOWER**
> Why, that I will.

By this point, the two characters are nose to nose. The older and wiser Glendower decides to back off from a fight, either because he knows that diplomacy is the only solution, or because he fears he might lose a fight against the younger, stronger Percy. It is up to the actors to search the text for clues as to how their characters might behave. I refer the players back to the original unedited text in the Folger edition, as well as the accompanying explanatory notes. If your group does not have access to the Folger edition, the complete text of every Shakespeare play is available for free on MIT's Shakespeare website (see appendix). I have provided the blocking for this scene based on how my group performed it. I encourage you and your players to mine the text and find your own variations. By doing so, you will gain a greater appreciation of and understanding for the subtle power dance between Glendower and Hotspur, and this scene will come alive.

As detailed in the "Performing Shakespeare" essay, performers and directors can use Wordle.net (http://www.wordle.net/create) to create a "word cloud" graphic that emphasizes which words appear with greatest frequency in a character's speech. By cutting and pasting all of Hotspur's and Glendower's words from the MIT script into Wordle, we discover the words Glendower uses most: English, earth, heaven, shapes, fiery, deep, come, cousin, speak, men, birth, wives. Hotspur's text emphasizes the following: Earth, shame, devil, truth, shook, rather, shame. Actors can now use this information to color their words and shape their characters. At first glance, the most striking contrast is Glendower's use of the word "heaven" compared to Hotspur's use of "devil." Actors can make many more discoveries about their characters by using this simple and elegant free tool.

The second half of the scene is also fun for young actors because it contains some suggestive talk, particularly from Hotspur. Once his wife enters, we see another side to his otherwise aggressive nature, as he happily exclaims, "Come Kate, thou art perfect in lying down." In performance, this elicited some encouraging vocal responses from the adolescent audience. Lady Percy reinforces Hotspur's likeable side, stroking his head affectionately as he rests it in her lap. She suggests that he is "altogether governed by humors." What others say about a Shakespearean character provides additional clues as to his nature—and allows us to a portray a three-dimensional living, breathing person, with faults as well as good qualities, i.e., someone like ourselves!

SCENE 5 (ACT III, SCENE II)

Interestingly, art imitated life in this short scene during our 2009 production of *Henry IV, Part 1*. The actor playing Hal in this scene had recently been expelled from school and then reinstated. He had just spent a lot of time apologizing for his behavior, and now he was playing a son apologizing for the same. Needless to say, I encouraged him to use recent occurrences as inspiration as his character begged for his father's pardon.

We do not always have the opportunity for the play's exact mirroring of our own experiences, but with a bit of searching, it is not difficult to find conflicts in our own lives or others' that are similar to those in Shakespeare's texts. Sometimes it takes imagination or a metaphorical leap. In this particular case, the young actor playing Hal simply had to act the same way he had been acting in his real life: genuinely contrite and apologetic. When he stood up and looked straight out at the audience, saying, "This, in the name of God, I promise here," I believed he meant it.

SCENE 6 (ACT V, SCENE IV)

The scene begins with two back-to-back fights, the first between Douglas and King Henry and the second between Hotspur and Hal. My colleague Michael Tolaydo, a professional actor, came in to choreograph these fights, and as a result, they were executed crisply, safely, and dramatically. With fight scenes, it is best to enlist the help of someone with experience in fight choreography. Too often I have seen student actors rush at each other, wooden swords in hand, without ample guidance. Safety first: if you cannot enlist the services of a professional, at least rehearse your fight scene slowly and with exact blocking so that actors are not hurt.

Due to the well-choreographed fight, the actors playing Hal and Hotspur are able to throw themselves into the swordplay with vigor. Hal emits what amounts to primal screams, to the audience's delight. When Falstaff enters, he and Hal indulge in a choreographed, multi-part secret handshake that the actors devised on their own, which goes far toward personalizing their relationship. The actor playing Falstaff contrived several other moves on his own, including a dramatic sheathing of both his and dead Hotspur's swords over his corpulent (pillow-stuffed) belly. When he states that he looks to be either "Earl or Duke, I can assure you," he stiffens proudly and poses in profile, using his own sword to knight himself.

Many of the best physicalizations come from the actors themselves. My job is to lay the groundwork for them to develop an understanding and enthusiasm for their roles, as well as the confidence in their own ability to bring their characters to life. This Falstaff was indeed a live one. As he waved his sword about him in a circle to illustrate the hour that he claimed to have been fighting Percy, his fat-pillow fell from under his shirt, to hysterical audience laughter. He simply went on with his speech, several pounds lighter, with the pillow laying helplessly inert on the stage. This is live theater. One must simply keep going.

SCENE 7 (ACT V, SCENE I)

This last scene is taken from *Henry IV, Part 2*. It is intended to show the rejection of Falstaff and to give actors and audience a glimpse of what is to come in Shakespeare's ongoing tale of a young king who grows up and must leave his past behind. It is a touching and painful scene, as King Henry (formerly Hal) not only shuns his old friend, but banishes Falstaff from within ten miles of him.

As described in the "Performing Shakespeare" essay, by drunkenly offering the King a sip from her character's flask, the actress playing Bardolph inadvertantly undermined the emotional punch of this scene. Thus instead of reacting to a poignant moment, the audience responded with laughter to a funny bit. This type of response during performance is not uncommon, especially with young audiences. If you are performing the play more than once in front of a live audience, you will have a chance to prepare your actors (although laughter may spring up at another unexpected moment during the next performance).

There is no secret answer to how to prevent the unexpected in theatre, nor are we guaranteed the audience response we desire. But by delving into the text, committing to the characters, and playing with passion, your group can deliver a production that not only brings joy and satisfaction to audiences, but also builds performers' confidence, opening them up to the vivid worlds that Shakespeare creates. At the end of the play, as the cast belts out Falstaff's speech on "honor" in a joyful call-and-response, the theater hall vibrates with the energy of a youthful cast, fully engaged in telling Shakespeare's story.

Live theater is magical. It is the most dynamic form of entertainment available to us. There is nothing like the interchange between actors and audience, that vibrant energy that is created in the theater. *Henry IV, Part 1* is a magnificent story of a young king and his friends—but it is also a story about how we all grow up and, in doing so, change. We are fortunate to be able to continue bringing this play to life, especially with young performers who can give it the vitality it deserves.

✶ *HENRY IV, PART 1:*
SET AND PROP LIST

SET PIECES:

Bench
Table
Two stools
Throne

PROPS:

SCENE 1:

Swords for Henry and Falstaff
Dagger for Falstaff
Pillow for Falstaff's big belly
Bottle or wineskin for Bardolph

SCENE 2

Money bag for travelers
Scarf to tie around Bardolph's mouth
Rope to tie up travelers
Swords for rogues

SCENE 3

Mugs for tavern revelers
Bottle of wine to fill mugs
Cushion for Falstaff's "crown"

SCENE 4

Rolled-up map for Glendower

SCENE 6

Swords for all

Henry IV, Part 1

By William Shakespeare

Folger Secondary School Shakespeare Festival

Tuesday, March 10th, 2009

Senior English Class | Instructor: Mr. Leo Bowman | Guest Director: Mr. Nick Newlin

Fight Choreography: Michael Tolaydo

CAST OF CHARACTERS:

Scene 1: (Act I Scene II)

Narrator: Kiera Grant
Falstaff: Imani Shanklin Roberts
Prince Henry (Hal): Noelle Davis
Poins: Ashley Walker-Smith
Peto: Keyanna Hymes
Bardolph: Meggan Thompson
Gadshill: Kelley Dove

Scene 2: (Act II scene II)

Narrator: Kiera Grant
Falstaff: Imani Shanklin Roberts
Prince Henry (Hal): Noelle Davis
Poins: Ashley Walker-Smith
Peto: Keyanna Hymes
Bardolph: Meggan Thompson
Gadshill: Kelley Dove
Traveler 1: Nebyu Mahtemework
Traveler 2: James Wrenn II

Scene 3 (Act II Scene IV)
Narrator: Brianna Vega
Falstaff: Imani Shanklin Roberts
Prince Henry (Hal): Najah Musa
Poins: Ashley Walker-Smith
Hostess: Kiera Grant Bardolph: Meggan Thompson
Peto: Keyanna Hymes
Gadshill: Kelley Dove

Scene 3 (Act III Scene I)

Narrator: Cynthia Mattison
Hotspur (Percy): Reggie Lewis Williams
Lady Percy: Alex Wash

Glendower: Mone't Kingwood
Mortimer: Vincent Sumbry
Lady Mortimer: Clarke Randolph

Scene 4 (Act III Scene ii)
Narrator: Yvonne Nash
King Henry IV: Brian Petty
Prince Henry (Hal): Nebyu Mahtemework
(Prince Henry Understudy): Kelley Dove

Scene 5: (Act V Scene IV)

Narrator: Keyanna Hymes
King Henry IV: Brian Petty
Prince Henry (Hal): Nebyu Mahtemework
(Prince Henry Understudy): Keyanna Hymes
Hotspur: Reggie Lewis Williams
Douglas: Brianna Vega
Falstaff: James Wrenn II
Lancaster: Kelley Dove

Scene 6: (Rejection scene *Henry IV pt. 2* Act V, Scene V, and Falstaff "honor" speech)

Narrator: Meggan Thompson
King Henry IV: Aisha Friday Falstaff: James Wrenn II
Shallow: Cynthia Mattison
Pistol: Yvonne Nash
Bardolph: Meggan Thompson
Lord Chief Justice: Keyanna Hymes
Assistant to King: Noelle Davis

"I'll so offend to make offense a skill;
Redeeming time when men think least I will."
Prince Henry

ADDITIONAL RESOURCES

SHAKESPEARE

Shakespeare Set Free: Teaching Romeo and Juliet, Macbeth and a Midsummer Night's Dream
Peggy O'Brien, Ed., Teaching Shakespeare Institute
Washington Square Press
New York, 1993

Shakespeare Set Free: Teaching Hamlet and Henry IV, Part 1
Peggy O'Brien, Ed., Teaching Shakespeare Institute
Washington Square Press
New York, 1994

Shakespeare Set Free: Teaching Twelfth Night and Othello
Peggy O'Brien, Ed., Teaching Shakespeare Institute
Washington Square Press
New York, 1995

The Shakespeare Set Free series is an invaluable resource with lesson plans, activites, handouts, and excellent suggestions for rehearsing and performing Shakespeare plays in a classroom setting.

ShakesFear and How to Cure It!
Ralph Alan Cohen
Prestwick House, Inc.
Delaware, 2006

The Friendly Shakespeare: A Thoroughly Painless Guide to the Best of the Bard
Norrie Epstein
Penguin Books
New York, 1994

Brush Up Your Shakespeare!
Michael Macrone
Cader Books
New York, 1990

Shakespeare's Insults: Educating Your Wit
Wayne F. Hill and Cynthia J. Ottchen
Three Rivers Press
New York, 1991

Practical Approaches to Teaching Shakespeare
Peter Reynolds
Oxford University Press
New York, 1991

Scenes From Shakespeare:
A Workbook for Actors
Robin J. Holt
McFarland and Co.
London, 1988

THEATER AND PERFORMANCE

Impro: Improvisation and the Theatre
Keith Johnstone
Routledge Books
London, 1982

A Dictionary of Theatre Anthropology:
The Secret Art of the Performer
Eugenio Barba and Nicola Savarese
Routledge
London, 1991

THEATER GAMES

Theatre Games for Young Performers
Maria C. Novelly
Meriwether Publishing
Colorado, 1990

Improvisation for the Theater
Viola Spolin
Northwestern University Press
Illinois, 1983

Theater Games for Rehearsal:
A Director's Handbook
Viola Spolin
Northwestern University Press
Illinois, 1985

101 Theatre Games for Drama
Teachers, Classroom Teachers
& Directors
Mila Johansen
Players Press Inc.
California, 1994

PLAY DIRECTING

Theater and the Adolescent Actor:
Building a Successful School Program
Camille L. Poisson
Archon Books
Connecticut, 1994

Directing for the Theatre
W. David Sievers
Wm. C. Brown, Co.
Iowa, 1965

The Director's Vision: Play Direction
from Analysis to Production
Louis E. Catron
Mayfield Publishing Co.
California, 1989

INTERNET RESOURCES

http://www.folger.edu
The Folger Shakespeare Library's
website has lesson plans, primary
sources, study guides, images,
workshops, programs for teachers
and students, and much more. The
definitive Shakespeare website for
educators, historians and all lovers
of the Bard.

http://www.shakespeare.mit.edu.
The Complete Works of
William Shakespeare.
All complete scripts for *The
30-Minute Shakespeare* series were
originally downloaded from this site
before editing. Links to other internet
resources.

http://www.LoMonico.com/
Shakespeare-and-Media.htm
http://shakespeare-and-media
.wikispaces.com
Michael LoMonico is Senior
Consultant on National Education
for the Folger Shakespeare Library.
His *Seminar Shakespeare 2.0* offers a
wealth of information on how to use
exciting new approaches and online
resources for teaching Shakespeare.

http://www.freesound.org.
A collaborative database of sounds
and sound effects.

http://www.wordle.net.
A program for creating "word clouds"
from the text that you provide. The
clouds give greater prominence to
words that appear more frequently in
the source text.

http://www.opensourceshakespeare
.org.
This site has good searching capacity.

http://shakespeare.palomar.edu/
default.htm
Excellent links and searches

http://shakespeare.com/
Write like Shakespeare,
Poetry Machine, tag cloud

http://www.shakespeare-online.com/

http://www.bardweb.net/

http://www.rhymezone.com/
shakespeare/
Good searchable word and phrase
finder.
Or by lines:
http://www.rhymezone.com/
shakespeare/toplines/

http://shakespeare.mcgill.ca/
Shakespeare and Performance
research team

http://www.enotes.com/william-
shakespeare

Needless to say, the internet goes on and on with valuable Shakespeare resources.
The ones listed here are excellent starting points and will set you on your way in the
great adventure that is Shakespeare.

NICK NEWLIN has been performing the comedy and variety act *Nicolo Whimsey* for international audiences for 25 years. Since 1996, he has conducted an annual play directing residency affiliated with the Folger Shakespeare Library in Washington, D.C. Newlin received a BA with Honors from Harvard University in 1982 and an MA in Theater with an emphasis in Play Directing from the University of Maryland in 1996.

THE 30-MINUTE SHAKESPEARE

All plays $7.95, available in bookstores everywhere

"Nick Newlin's 30-minute play cuttings are perfect for students who have no experience with Shakespeare. Each 30-minute mini-play is a play in itself with a beginning, middle, and end." —Michael Ellis-Tolaydo, Department of Theater, Film, and Media Studies, St Mary's College of Maryland

PHOTOCOPYING AND PERFORMANCE RIGHTS